how to join the club of the rich and famous!
a short guide to social climbing

*This book is dedicated to
my grandfather, Theodore,
who thought that public notoriety
and self-promotion were
commonplace and
who epitomised good taste.
And to my son Nicholas who,
I hope, will grow up to be like him.*

how to join the club of the rich and famous!

a short guide to social climbing

valentina artsrunik

ARTNIK • LONDON

First published in Great Britain in 2003
by Artnik
26 Pont Street
London SW1X 0AB
England

This is a revised edition of an earlier book, *How to become rich and (in)famous – the definitive shortcut!*

© Valentina Artsrunik 2003

All rights reserved. No part of this publication may be reproduced, stored in or introduced into a retrieval system, or transmitted in any form or by any means (electronic, mechanical, photocopying, recording or otherwise) without the prior written permission of both the copyright owner and the publisher of this book.

ISBN 1 903906 01 6

Cartoons: Peter Heaton
Design: Linda Wade
Editor: Elizabeth Shaw-Hardie

Printed and bound in Bulgaria by Demax plc

contents

Foreword	7
Introduction	9
Define the Goal	11
Invent a New Persona	13
Party, Party, Party…	23
On Parade	55
Migrate with the Jet Set	76
If all else fails…	85
Final Words of Wisdom	109

Acknowledgements and Credits

Nicholas Artsrunik is my photographer and computer assistant.

Vanko Djelebov took 'the devil out' of the logistics details.

Alexenia Dimitrova inspired the idea.

Peter McCloud showed me kindness and integrity when both mattered critically.

Derek Alexander has been a long time legal adviser beyond the call of duty.

John Zwerling and Lisa Kemler saved me from the brink of utter disaster.

foreword

It is delightful to hear that the most 'infamous' of my closest friends has written this entertaining investigative exploration into what makes the rich and famous tick, how they got there, and what they do with their notoriety. Valentina is an inspiration to those who might aspire to follow in their steps. The world would be a duller place if they all ceased their activities and suddenly became 'normal', perhaps even coming to personify the height of respectability!

Alexander Thynn,
Marquess of Bath

Spring 2003

Fame is not contagious and wealth does not rub off. You have to create your own.

introduction

This short and concise guide has been inspired by several newspaper, magazine and TV interviews, in the course of which the author has been asked to comment on various aspects of marrying well, building an individual style, courting publicity; to define the ingredients of those intangible qualities – elegance, distinction and charm; and to disclose the trendy destinations to travel to and meet other successful and fascinating people, and so on.

This guide aims to unravel some of the above and to explore a strategy of 'getting there'. It is written humorously – tongue in cheek – as the subject does not bear being taken very seriously, but it contains many a grain of wisdom, acquired in the course of vast personal experience and observation.

Wealth and celebrity are the hallmarks of success – or

so the media, which feeds off both, has us believe. So, how does one get there, without being armed with the proverbial silver spoon at birth?

> *Determination and lack of scruples help, as does luck, but a shortcut requires strategy, and this is what we will explore in this book.*

The following chapters aim to help the reader establish the credentials necessary to join the circles of people who possess wealth or notoriety, or both. These credentials are some of the tools that are needed to build fame and fortune.

Fame is not contagious and wealth does not rub off. You have to create your own.

Valentina Artsrunik
Spring 2003

define the goal

Whether you are young and full of hope, or middle-aged and disenchanted with your existence, choosing your direction constitutes base one in the pursuit of that elusive nirvana – success, as measured by the yardstick of your peers.

Hard work and industriousness, integrity and career devotion can, and often do, mean plodding and 'kissing' some apparatchik's posterior. Besides, a salary rise does not get your smiling face on the front page of the Daily Celebrity News and your party frock or waistcoat discussed by morning TV's fashion editor.

That said, the truly vastly rich lurk in the twilight: they do not like to grace the pages of various gossip sheets. More on that subject in another chapter, but suffice to say that even if you enlist the complicity of a diarist in your quest for notoriety, you must at least pretend not to enjoy the limelight, and certainly you must not appear to hanker after it.

The truly famous are well aware of another truism – the more you hanker after publicity the more it eludes you, which is why they employ public relations consultants to do the hankering for them.

The first step towards joining the ranks of the rich and famous – if you have set this as your definite goal – is to persuade them that you are one of them. Like any other club, this one is exclusive, but not as exclusive as its members would have you believe.

inventing a new persona

Consider this scenario: you have been invited or decided to go to the races. The safest dress code dictates a tweedy suit for both men and women, a sensible hat, equally sensible shoes or boots, and perhaps also a pair of binoculars to follow the race. A safely married countrified matron or the ageing daughter of a peer would adopt this together with a string of pearls. A younger and more daring version of the above would opt for trousers and a trendy top.

You want to be noticed but not to stand out for your garishness. Forget the tartan and pearls, forget the trend of the moment. From your mid-twenties onwards you will have established what suits you – or you should have. Pick the colour that sets off the colour of your eyes or hair. Emphasise your best feature. Then dress in that colour, adopting the cut that flatters your figure the most.

HOW TO JOIN THE CLUB OF RICH AND FAMOUS

Do not be superfluous. Make a bold but spare statement. If your colour is blue, wear a bright, self-coloured blue outfit paired with an interesting hat (if you are able to wear hats with the confidence they require), and a stylish accessory – an oversized handkerchief, or perhaps even gloves . A monocle or a pair of opera glasses to study the form is far better by way of sartorial statement than any trendy label.

You are in pursuit of wealth and fame – you wish to consort with those who have already 'arrived' so that you can get there yourself and be perceived as one of them. It is an old truism that people lend only to those who are rich. It follows that image is vital.

Reinventing oneself is nothing new, but finding a persona to fit the desired image is what most people fail at. If one is not already rich and well known, one needs to acquire the attributes, mannerisms and confidence of such a person – in short, one needs to establish a credible presence.

INVENTING A NEW PERSONA

If your outfit is striking or original enough and your manner confident you might get photographed by a Vogue *snapper.*

Not all rich people are educated, but virtually all of them have either sought to improve themselves or were born into a social class in which education in academic terms is not of utmost relevance. A congenial manner, regard for etiquette and ritual, a certain awareness of current affairs, as well as the

ability to express oneself and engage in social banter, all go a long way to masking shortcomings in one's education. There is no masking poor locution, however. The only available option for a poorly spoken person is to pretend to be a foreigner. However, while a foreigner is forgiven for lacking in his expression, he is not excused if he is lacking in his manners.
First impressions are often vital, especially in these days of breathless pace and disposable friendships. Before you even open your mouth, you are judged by your general appearance.

Making an entrance places you on the map instantly. People who wear designer clothes let the labels verify their status. If you cannot afford couture or daren't be original buy second-hand Chanel, YSL, Prada, etc., and no one will be any the wiser if you wear them with panache.

A friend of mine, whose husband is a Hong Kong tycoon and who can afford the most fantastically expensive couture gowns, frequently turns up at parties wearing simple label-less garments she might have purchased in her native Turkey. Her style, beauty

INVENTING A NEW PERSONA

and confidence set her apart. As a housekeeper of mine once remarked, 'You could buy a $10 dress and people would think it costs $1,000. I could wear a $1,000 dress and people would think I've paid a tenner for it.'

The next best thing to designer labels is individuality. Go for well-cut one off garments that spell confidence. Second-hand and charity shops in wealthy areas are a source of countless bargains if carefully scouted. Good-quality pre-1960s clothes are achieving new heights of prominence these days under the guise of 'vintage clothing'. You can go to well-established shops such as Steinberg & Tolkien or rummage through city flea markets and provincial charity shops. However, you do need unerring taste, conviction and confidence to achieve an interesting, rather than a frumpy, look.

Designer jewellery on the other hand is altogether different. It does not date. It appreciates in value and can represent a formidable investment unlike high-street gold and diamond trinkets. Collecting Cartier, Fabergé, Tiffany, Bulgari, Van Cleef & Arpels shows sublime taste and perspicacity. Take the time and effort to study the different styles of the great jewellers of our times. A man is likely to offer such a gift only to a woman capable of appreciating it. Better to wear a simple Cartier pendant at all times than to sport countless gold chains or large nondescript baubles.

All jewellery designers have developed a range of accessories. A silver scent bottle that fits into a purse, a silver cigarette case or compact sets you apart in ways that an expensive frock alone cannot. After all, others might have purchased the exact same dress.

Accessories, in fact, are as important as clothes. A Hermés scarf or a Louis Vuitton handbag add a touch of distinction. But it is far better not to possess one than to acquire a cheap fake in New York's China Town.

Copying may be the cheapest form of flattery, but it is just that – cheap.

Similarly, it is better to wear no scent at all than to reek of cheap perfume.

INVENTING A NEW PERSONA

My personal favourites – established after years of trying every new fragrance on the market – are the delicate lily-of-the-valley-based Christian Dior scents and Hermés' 24 Faubourg.

So, you have made a memorable entrance. How do you capitalise on the moment? If your outfit is striking enough and your manner confident you might get photographed by a *paparazzo*. Make sure he gets your name correctly, and spare a friendly word for him – chances are, you will come across him again. He doesn't decide whose picture gets published, but he can decide whose face gets snapped.

You must devote a great deal of thought to your first appearance at a social/sporting/cultural event. That appearance will henceforth be a part of your persona – the image you wish to project to the world you are striving to join. Whether classic and demure, or eccentric and flamboyant, you need to work hard at maintaining the image so as to impress yourself on a fickle public.

If originality in dress is matched by originality of

opinion, expression and thought then you are halfway there. You are your greatest asset. Tell yourself this and use it. Be charming and witty so that you represent desirable company.

The PR Consultant

The pulse of the socially aware beats through an invisible web of connections that are largely provided and exploited by that mighty fixer of our times, the Public Relations Consultant.

There are two breeds of PR consultant.
There are the Max Cliffords of this world – professionals, whose symbiosis with the media creates apocryphal stories, or keeps very important ones out of the public gaze. Such consultants have counterparts in just about every country in the world, but are particularly prolific in America where they are called publicists.

Then there are the Liz Brewers – old-school well-born hostesses who have used their address books to

INVENTING A NEW PERSONA

fashion a living. They are retained by foreign tycoons who want to break onto the social scene effortlessly and are prepared to pay for the service.
There is a core ageing rent-a-crowd in every large city, whose members are only too happy to swap an evening of watching TV for a couple of hours drinking champagne and chatting with chums while pretending to admire the latest jeweller's wares.

There are also the 'people launchers', among whom Martine Montgomery has carved an honorary place by gist of creating the modern 'IT Girl' phenomenon.

Young aristocrats aspiring to turn their social connections into business portfolios, middle-aged hostesses with much time on their hands, and media executives with a wealth of accounts – any of them could and do turn their hand to PR at one time or another. To some it comes naturally because they have been brought up to socialise. To others it's a fun networking job that leads to other ventures – or marriage.

A PR is only as good as his or her address book.

So, the best option for any hopeful *R&F* (rich and famous person) is to cultivate two distinctly different types of PR consultant: a professional one who has access to and influence over the media and a trendy one who counts among his/her friends the faces of the moment – an eclectic mixture of pop stars, actors and sundry celebrities, as well as young heirs to old titles.

If you cannot afford to hire a PR, befriend one: take him or her to lunch, send some flowers or cigars, a bottle of wine or other small gift; make a gesture, no matter how trite – above all, flatter them.

> *We are all susceptible to flattery. Tell them they are the best and that is why you want to be friends with them.*

party, party, party...

There are several types of function, and keeping your social diary full is essential if you are to achieve *R&F* status. However, there are various codes of behaviour that you will have to become familiar with if you want to be accepted within the party set.

There are universal rules that pertain to good taste, but etiquette is especially important when one is invited to a private reception.

At most social gatherings nowadays, it is all right to introduce yourself to other people. This is especially true if the function is a charity or political fundraiser.

Indeed, you are expected to circulate and talk to strangers, or your hostess will feel compelled to take care of you – a sin she will not forgive lightly. Finding yourself at a party and spending the entire evening with your partner or, God forbid, the same person who first had the misfortune of greeting you, is a capital faux pas – a no no.

As you move around, talking to different guests, you need to use a great deal of charm and flattery.

Be sure you know what the correct form of address is. If in doubt, wait for one of your peers to address the person concerned, and then follow suit. In these egalitarian days most people adopt the use of first names shortly after introduction, but polite society requires an awareness at least of correctness.

Think of current topics of conversation, but do not express extreme opinions as they might offend. Controversial topics are usually proposed by the host or hostess in order to enliven the conversation and give it an edge. Be bold, but only if you know your subject.

A hostess worth her salt will have invited at least one eccentric, controversial guest to provide some of the

PARTY, PARTY, PARTY...

excitement – either by virtue of his or her wit, humour, erudition, attire, or all of these put together.

There is an acceptable level of name-dropping that establishes belonging to the same circle. Use the name of a common acquaintance, no matter how trivial, especially if you know the name carries weight.

If you have had the opportunity of meeting the social diarist Nigel Dempster, for example, you could simply use his name to open conversation.

Be charming to members of your own gender. Most rich and famous people are attached, and their partners do not appreciate blatant flirting: they are likely to blackball you if they suspect you are a spouse/girlfriend/boyfriend poacher.

In fact, flirting is one area of social discourse that can prove something of a minefield to the uninitiated. While blatant flirting smacks of vulgarity, there is the acceptable, indeed prerequisite, social flirting. The latter is a form of art, cultivated among the well bred as a matter of course and etiquette.

HOW TO JOIN THE CLUB OF RICH AND FAMOUS

Many a hostess enjoys playing a matchmaking game, even with married men and women. Thus over the years I have been encouraged to flirt with a succession of rich older guests on whose return hospitality certain hostesses counted.

There is absolutely nothing wrong with asking a well-married friend to introduce you to an eligible bachelor or single lady. The idle rich love matchmaking and, besides, such a request will reassure the friend that you have not set your sights on his or her own spouse.

> *If you are a single woman forget about political correctness altogether – wealthy men prefer old-fashioned girls who can play the piano, arrange flowers and look exquisite, rather than nurse important careers of their own. They like attention.*

Fasten onto your interlocutor as if he were the most fascinating person you have ever come across; and tell him so too. If you are truly interested in him, make

PARTY, PARTY, PARTY…

him feel important and clever. Do not ask a man how old he is or how he has made his fortune. Do not play hard to get. Be feminine, not politically correct.

If you are a single man, do not ask a woman what she does for a living – *ladies do not work*. They sometime have careers, but if that is the case they will volunteer the information.

If the conversation turns to age, imply that you think them ten years younger than what you suspect they are (unless they are in their twenties still) – never ever ask even an oblique question pertaining to age.

Show appreciation for her taste and intelligence. The prettier the woman, the more insecure she feels and the more she craves being taken seriously. Few of us are secure enough not to need flattery.

Remember to tell the hostess how delightful the flower arrangements are, how generous her hospitality, how elegant, slim and beautiful she looks, and what an unerring taste she has in decorating the house. You must use the most suitable superlatives (naturally, you cannot tell a fat woman that she looks slim) and tell people what they like to hear, even if you do not mean any of it.

Always say 'beautiful' when you mean pretty; 'absolutely delicious' when you mean adequate; 'perfectly charming' when you mean not bad; 'frightfully busy' when you mean a fairly full diary, and so on.

The Launch Party

The most common function is the launch or promotional party.

Usually organised by a professional PR, this type of function is considered to be the great equaliser. When a newcomer hits London or New York, and they want to launch a product (often the 'product' is themselves), they hire a PR to give them instant notoriety.

If they happen to be Ivana Trump they go for Liz Brewer – the doyenne of 'old money meets new'

PARTY, PARTY, PARTY...

society – and pay for a tailor-made circle of friends and acquaintances. So overwhelming can the number of introductions be that the person thus launched exists in permanent confusion as to whom they have met or have yet to meet.

To illustrate the point, I once approached Ivana Trump at the restaurant San Lorenzo and introduced her to a friend of mine (male) who was dying to meet her. I had encountered Trump only briefly at a party and was quite certain that she wouldn't have a clue who I was. She nevertheless greeted me as a long lost friend and promised to 'do lunch' with me 'a.s.a.p., darling'.

A PR is most often retained to launch a shop or a restaurant or a hotel – even a new scent. Depending on the PR 's address book and the time of the year (sought-after guests can contemplate several functions in any one night during the 'season'), one encounters the most eclectic mixture of people at such parties. Ancient aristocrats, and even minor royalty (especially exiled royalty), rub shoulders with starlets, arm dealers from Eastern Europe, American tycoons and their latest wives (themselves ranging from former soft-porn actresses to successful career women), film producers, gossip writers, and a generous sprinkling of wannabes who have somehow made it to the guest list.

Most of the grandees tend to consort with each other and ignore the commoners – or those that they perceive as commonplace. But none is averse to partaking of the hospitality extended – whether it is offered by a mid-European jeweller, or a young restaurateur, or an art importer.

This is the ground where new connections are built, and even though the business card is frowned upon by the old guard a hopeful *R&F* should carry a plentiful supply and hand one to every willing recipient. You never know – the next person might be a hopeful PR consultant.

If you are already rich, you can become famous and fêted almost overnight, simply by purchasing – at any cost and with good grace – whatever it is that is being launched. PRs would fall over themselves to add you to their lists, and even old grandees, who are not immune to greed, would smile upon you – perhaps condescendingly at first, but in earnest as you extend your generosity to them.

Auction Houses and Galleries

The auction house preview is the next type of function to aim for. Bluff your way on to their invitation lists (which do not change for years) and then stay there by hook or by crook. Auction houses give regular parties to highlight a forthcoming sale or just thank their long-term patrons. In order to get yourself on the invitation list (and once on it, you remain on it), you can try one of several things.

The most obvious is to get to know someone who works at Christie's or Sotheby's. You might consider a short art appreciation course (run by the auction house). Or you might attend regular auctions (which are free) and register your particular interest with the department you want to be associated with. Entering low bids from time to time legitimises your interest.

Gate-crashing a cocktail party (having seen an

invitation on someone else's mantelpiece) is another course of action. This requires great panache, however. If challenged, you should be able to feign misplacing the card and to produce a suitably grand name or title to assuage the suspicions of the receptionists. Do sign your full name and address on the book. Even if you give a false name, always give the correct address: postmen deliver to the address, not necessarily the addressee. Chances are you will be invited the next time.

Like auction house previews, gallery openings are the easy pick-up territory of the society crowd. Tax exiles, too old for night clubs, hunt there for discreet companions; bored middle-aged women look for excitement; artists look for commissions; and collectors look for new talent.

Roy Miles, who threw the best gallery openings in London in the 1980s, recognised the powerful social appeal of these soirées and made the most of it. One lustful old roué, an expatriate, bought countless Russian pictures from the Roy Miles gallery – out of a sense of 'social obligation' and because he recruited many of his youthful paramours in the course of such excursions. The girls may have long gone but he is probably in possession of a formidable collection…

It is as well to keep track of who is buying at such events – a word of admiration for their good taste goes a long way to demonstrating shared interest and offers an opening to leaving that business card. But do be aware of the spouse. I once struck up an innocent conversation in front of a picture I admired. The man with whom I was conversing – a media tycoon – was promptly whisked off by a furious-looking female. She went on to marry him, but hasn't stopped watching…

Charity Fundraiser

The charity fundraiser is a purely social phenomenon. It has nothing whatever to do with philanthropy, which is anonymous at best, discreet at worst. It has everything to do with power broking, one-upmanship, positioning for obtaining valuable social introductions, and acquiring credibility and a degree of prominence.

I know many whose entire social life revolves around

charity parties and who would be quite friendless if it were not for the charity circuit. It is absolutely the easiest and least expensive way to latch onto that bandwagon chugging on the road to notoriety if not fame. There are, nonetheless, rules to be observed here, too.

> *Make up your mind to throw your support behind a prestigious charity – one that has royal patronage and commands the best venues.*

Take time to study the names on the committees. Do not assume that you will be sitting next to all the titles on the stationery once you've joined a committee. The 'titles' lend their names to attract 'slaves' (people who do the work) and sponsors (those who foot the bill for anything from flowers to event programmes). Look for names of people that habitually grace the gossip columns.

Businessmen might not go to committee meetings, but they do go to the ball – and bring many of their clients along.

PARTY, PARTY, PARTY...

Once you have chosen your charity, find the local chapter and write a nice letter (handwritten with a fountain pen makes the best impression). If you are not certain of your ability to write letters, consult Debrett's *Guide to Etiquette and Modern Manners* or ask someone who knows and can advise you properly. Avoid asking to join a committee, at least to begin with – it is far better to be invited. Rather, imply that you have time on your hands and have been involved in charity fundraising before (be vague if this is not quite the case) and that you would like to help with their next fundraising effort and attend a fundraising event. You will get by return their calendar of events.

This is the moment to invest in your future as a *R&F* person, for no one has reaped dividends without investing first. The cost of a ticket for an event can range from a modest £10 to a small fortune if the Prince of Wales is putting in a presence, no matter how brief.

Of course, if you are already rich and merely need to become famous, all you need to do is make a sizeable donation to

*the relevant charity and then,
after a decent period of time,
you can make your yacht,
plane, chateau, island – whatever it is –
available to either a member
of the Royal Family or a member of
Senate, whichever is your preference.*

You are likely to be deemed suitable to join a committee if one of the following applies:

> You have given reason to be believed resourceful and hardworking when it comes to selling tickets.

> You are inventive where approaching advertisers/ sponsors is concerned.

> You have many friends whom you can persuade to attend events.

> You are effervescent, congenial, and of good background, and thus an asset to the group of event organisers.

PARTY, PARTY, PARTY...

You have connections within the media world and can attract publicity.

If all else fails, you can always ask to stand for a place on the committee. It is difficult to turn down a volunteer, although I have witnessed a power struggle within a certain charity committee that would have put any corporate board of directors' war to shame.

It is important to defer to senior and titled members of the committee. I made an early mistake of feeling over confident and dismissing a venerable lady who chaired a certain charity committee once. I was promptly expelled with a handwritten letter – polite but quite devastating.

Once on the committee, you can start networking. Apply yourself and within months you can acquire a circle of acquaintances, many of whom get their pictures in the newspapers.

Your social status will rise proportionately with the number of charities you support and the number of tickets you buy.

Thus, bemused Londoners saw the vertiginous rise (and equally vertiginous fall) of a certain Douglas 'Baron' McDillen about a decade ago. DD went around town purchasing an extraordinary number of tickets, bidding for most auction prizes, and lunching and dining with the high and mighty; in no time, he became the darling of London society. Alas, he ran out of cash and his newly acquired 'friends' dropped him faster than you can spell Baron.

The Party Political Fundraiser

Most people who acquire wealth put it to use in obtaining power or, at the very least, influencing those in power. Few rich people are content with sitting back and simply enjoying their good fortune. They want to meddle, they want to be in the forefront where their ideas can be heard and reckoned with, and they want to have recognition, be it in the form of titles or in the patronage of a politician they can lobby while entertaining him or her in their opera box.

If you would like to rub shoulders with this kind of social animal as well as with their beneficiaries –

PARTY, PARTY, PARTY...

sundry politicians – you need first to examine your political affiliations. If you have none, and all you are really seeking is the kudos from such association, you would do best to court the party currently in power (although there is a lot to be said for going for the underdog).

It used to be that the well-to-do supported the Conservatives (or the Republicans in the United States). But the boundaries have become so blurred – now that politicians pander to cash contributors, pressure groups and the media – that wealthy individuals are constantly switching allegiances according to which side catches them first or cultivates them more assiduously.

I know one lucratively divorced *demi-mondaine* who expends an inordinate amount of time and money working tirelessly for her local Conservative Association. Her teenage son gets to offer his teachers books personally signed by a former prime minister. His mother, though, is eyeing the ultimate reward – this plump, middle-aged lady is consumed by exalted aspirations of becoming a Dame at least and given a peerage at best.

To join either side of the political divide, all you need to do is call your local party association and express an interest in the fundraising events calendar. You might be asked to go stuffing envelopes once a year, or even door to door canvassing. Do it. Both are fun, and a gregarious exercise to boot, and you get to meet lots of jolly people in the process.

If you have a large garden throw it open once a year for a cocktail party. I once had a friend who gave two parties a year – a private one and a political fundraiser. She told me that she got her year's invitations on the strength of that limited but well-calculated generosity.

> *Never ever lose sight of where you are heading.*

Every so often, a grand hostess will open her drawing room for a political gathering. Ticket prices will be steep to reflect the honour and the presence of an illustrious politician. The rich and the powerful will gravitate towards her salon, and you want to be there

PARTY, PARTY, PARTY...

at that exact time – business cards at the ready and your most charming smile in place.

There is a myriad of lobby groups and associations that are very often nothing more than a political springboard for an aspiring politician. The best example that comes to mind is a certain peer's daughter's pro-NATO group whose supporters are really supporting the lady herself. Happy to be associated with an earl's daughter, they fork out £40 or more on a regular basis so that they can sit at her dining room table and listen to a speaker she has managed to persuade to give an after-dinner speech. To her credit, these speakers are political wits who have already 'arrived' rather than being on the way up.

She is by no means the only one of the kind. The Countryside Alliance is a much larger and better-defined lobby organisation whose message has broader appeal.

In America such groups are too numerous to name – the Impeach Clinton.Org, a relative newcomer, was quite popular at the height of the Monica Lewinsky scandal, whereas the pro-gun NRA (National Rifle Association) has grass-root support that is second to none. The smaller the group, the more exclusive it is likely to be, and the better the chance of meeting *R&F* people you wish to consort with.

> *It is worth remembering that very few wealthy individuals would support a Marxist lobby group any more than a fur-clad lady would the support the anti-fur lobby.*

Sporting Events

An inordinate amount of literature has been devoted to the sporting event as a means of meeting eligible bachelors or girls about town.

It is relatively easy to put in a regular appearance at low-profile sporting events. Those favoured by the *R&F* are, in addition to polo, racing, shooting, sailing, tennis, and motor racing.

If you can afford to take up riding, deer stalking,

PARTY, PARTY, PARTY...

shooting, playing tennis, skiing, and racing cars, so much the better. Failing that, you have to content yourself with being a spectator.

If betting on horses has a somewhat populist and tarnished image (when it is done through a betting shop), going to the races, with its associated rituals, is *de rigueur* if you are a serious *R&F* pretender. There is a special etiquette associated with the races, and a lot of it you can glean from Debrett's *Guide to Etiquette and Modern Manners*, or some similar bible of good form.

The main racing events in England draw such vast numbers of spectators that it is worth going to Ascot, for example, only if you can make it to the Royal Enclosure. It is not true that getting an access voucher is next to impossible. You need to apply to the Steward and fill in an application form with the appropriate fee early in the year. You also need to find a sponsor who has been in the Royal Enclosure at least twice.

If you have gone through the motions described

HOW TO JOIN THE CLUB OF RICH AND FAMOUS

earlier in this guide, you should know at least two people who qualify. Cajole them until they sponsor your application. After the initiation, you are in, and can purchase vouchers for subsequent events as you would caviar from Harrods.

The racing season kicks off with the Derby. There is no Royal Enclosure at the Derby but there is a members' enclosure, and the only way you can gain access to it is if you know a member of the Jockey Club (one needs to be an owner in order to maintain membership of the Jockey Club).

Glorious Goodwood in August is more democratic but equally grand. Then, there are the lesser race meetings, totally ignored by the publications listing social events. But it is at these that one is most likely to strike a friendship (or find romance) with members of the select set. All you need to attend is a car, the small admission fee, and a certain air of knowing what you are doing. Study the form, look at the horses before they start racing, have a glass of wine at the bar, take a pair of binoculars and cheer the winner. (You never know, you might even be cheering the

PARTY, PARTY, PARTY…

horse you picked…) Remember, your attire must reflect the occasion. Splendour at Ascot, but low-key tweeds and rubber boots at lesser events.

If you cannot afford deer stalking or real safari, you can always take up clay-pigeon shooting. Holland&Holland give courses on the outskirts of London, and there are plenty of shooting clubs and ranges elsewhere. Since it is an élitist sport in most of Europe it can be cheaper to learn to handle a weapon on another continent before showing off your marksmanship in Europe.

Polo has its own calendar and you can spend several months of each year following it from country to country. They even have polo on ice in St Moritz. (St Moritz also hosts a unique sporting event incidentally – the Cresta Run – which is as exclusive as it is dare-devilish. There is more about this in the travel section.) The late Susan Barrantes gave a whole new meaning to 'treading the field' at polo matches (when the spectators help to press back pieces of turf churned up by the horses' feet). Some pretty famous romantic matches have been made while treading between chukkas or drinking Pimms after the match.

If you want an effortless entrée into the polo set, you would be well advised to cultivate some superior Indian connections. The Rajmata of Jaipur is the undisputed doyenne of the sport, and wherever she goes a flock of aristocratic Indians follow in the wake.

Riding and sailing are sports that one usually takes up when still young. Both are difficult to master in later life, but by no means impossible. Men and women born to wealth have been instructed in both as surely as they have been instructed in reading. You can take a sailing course in London for around £300 and then join a yacht as crew for a month or so. You won't get paid unless you are experienced, but you might meet some interesting people and perfect your skills. The experience might also give you a conversation topic second to none.

Riding can be learnt at an equestrian centre or riding school, and a few intensive lessons should enable you to feel confident enough to mount a horse every now and then, though not for riding to hounds. Riding to hounds (i.e. hunting) is for the landed gentry and members of riding clubs. Generally, you need to have wealth – or hunting friends – to indulge in it regularly.

Chances are you will have played tennis at school. Keep it up as often as you can. It is a great sport and often engaged in during visits to country estates. If you have never skied in your youth, you are in for a surprise. It is a physically demanding sport. You can learn the basics in a couple of weeks by going to some inexpensive country such as Bulgaria; you can then invest in a week in Gstaad where you can rub shoulders with beautiful people. (More about that in travel.)

Embassy and Cultural Events

Embassy and cultural events can be identical, which is why I shall discuss them in one section.
Embassy receptions are given usually in order to promote their country's culture or economy. You need to have some important association with a particular country to find yourself on the invitation list. Failing that, you need a journalist friend to take you along.

HOW TO JOIN THE CLUB OF RICH AND FAMOUS

Many years ago, I was taken by a senior BBC reporter to a reception at the Bulgarian Embassy, given in honour of Robert Maxwell, the late media tycoon, who had just published an encyclopaedia-like book on the country. Two days later I was having dinner with Maxwell at his favourite casino, Maxim's.

The US Embassy in London holds particularly enchanting events for expatriates and sundry lovers of America, as well as for the media. If you can get on their list you are assured of meeting some interesting people and having a great time along the way. I was fortunate enough to be invited to a couple of parties given by Raymond Seitz (who was then US Ambassador in London); a genial and distinguished host, he was extremely well liked both for his charm and for his delightful sense of mischief.

Ambassadors do not come any better bred than G. W. Bush's choice of envoy to the Court of St James's in London. William Stamps Farish III brings opulence and distinction to diplomatic and sporting events alike. As a personal friend of the Queen, he should feel entirely in his element, and an invitation from him and his wife

PARTY, PARTY, PARTY...

will be greatly sought after in the next few years.

Gallery openings, art talks, literary lunches, operatic and theatrical events – all of these are the stamping ground of rich and cultured philanthropists. The opera (Glyndebourne falls into this category although it has become a corporate hospitality event of late) and the theatre can be expensive. The sensible thing to do if you cannot afford good seats is to buy the cheapest ticket and visit the stalls' drinking area during the intervals. With some perseverance and luck you could find yourself moving within the heady world of art sponsors and donors.

Opportunities are there to be taken all the time – identifying them and seizing them is the difficult part for most people.

The Private Reception

If you have followed this guide at least in part, you should have 'graduated' to receiving some invitations to private receptions. While these have the merit of being free – you do not have to buy a ticket to attend

– you will certainly be expected to reciprocate either by giving your own party or, if you are a bachelor, inviting your hosts to the theatre or a restaurant or both.

There are many tiers to the private party.
It can be a cocktail party or a dinner party. It can be a small informal reception or a formal one to celebrate/commemorate/launch something or other.

By definition the rich and famous give mostly formal parties, complete with a magazine photographer who records the proceedings for posterity and makes it possible for the host and hostess to add to their scrapbook of glittering celebrity press.

I will describe one particular formula here that many Londoners of a certain age will recognise. The formula was invented by a former friend of mine who was briefly mentioned earlier. A single woman for decades, she choose to give one reception every year. To this she invited not only all of her old friends and those she had made in the course of the previous year but all those who were likely to be hosting their own receptions in the near future or who might invite her

PARTY, PARTY, PARTY...

to some exotic location. As she could not afford (or was not willing) to feed all these guests (about 300 of them each year), she persuaded some twenty of them to have their own dinner party prior to her party and to invite to this dinner party about a dozen of the guests from her master list. All 300 or so invitees arrived after dinner at her house for drinks and dancing (it helped, of course, that she had a rather large house in Cheyne Walk). This party was purely strategic in concept and had nothing to do with the hostess's generosity.

There are, as ever, a number of rules to observe with private parties:

> 1. Never refuse an invitation – you never know whom you might meet there. If you decide it is a third-rate party, you can leave after half an hour or so without causing offence.

> 2. Never take a companion unless it has been specified that you may. Singles are highly prized by hostesses – especially straight single men. A hostess will arrange

HOW TO JOIN THE CLUB OF RICH AND FAMOUS

> a party around equal numbers of men and women and will never forgive you if you call to beg for your latest date to be included. It is bad form, anyway.

If you are a single man, and a suave and charming one at that, you could easily join the private party circuit by becoming a 'walker'.

A walker is a gentleman who escorts ladies to parties that they do not wish to attend unaccompanied. His duties stop there.

PARTY, PARTY, PARTY...

A walker is a gentleman (as opposed to a gigolo) who escorts ladies of a certain age to parties that they do not wish to attend unaccompanied.

While it is perfectly acceptable for a man to go by himself, a single woman is frowned upon, unless she is exceptionally attractive and has been invited specifically as bait to another guest.

Finally, never let a day elapse, post party, without sending a handwritten thank-you letter, some flowers if you have been invited to dinner, or a box of chocolates or dried fruit.

Cultivate a Gossip/Society Writer

Society columnists, lesser diarists and sundry gossip writers rule supreme in the world of media-generated celebrity. PR consultants rely on them for exposure, and gossip writers rely on PRs for information. It is a relationship that works well and can create an overnight celebrity.

Bienvenida Buck hired Max Clifford, who made her

notorious and rich in a matter of days. Such notoriety is short-lived, however. Not that many people have staying power, and when they do they owe it more to their personal style than to a particular columnist or PR, but the latter two are the instrument that shapes the scandal we are all so partial to.

on parade

Now, you may think that your life story has the hallmark of a Hollywood movie. It may be that you have indeed a fascinating story to tell… The world will only hear about it if a reporter (a celebrity reporter at that) decides to tell it to the world. The media is capricious and obeys its own laws.

Essentially, there are many stories out there and it is up to an editor to decide which one is newsworthy. If a story threatens to upset a major advertiser or another publisher, its merits will be closely weighed. If it is damaging to an existing celebrity, its publication would depend on the relationship that the celebrity's PR has with the particular newspaper.

Many a great story has not been told because it was deemed unnewsworthy by an editor.

HOW TO JOIN THE CLUB OF RICH AND FAMOUS

Richard Desmond, the very controversial and occasionally maligned owner and publisher of *OK* magazine and the *Daily Express* (the two best known among his sundry publications), has an undeniable flair where the celebrity-hungry market is concerned.

There are, of course, the legends among society or gossip writers who have discretion on what and whom they write about. They are accountable only to the publication's lawyers, who always demand hard copy proof. So you cannot invent some wild story that would propel you instantly into the realm of stardom. You have to be able to back it up.

If you cannot get an introduction to the gossip writer of your choice, the next best thing is to try a bit of flattery – again! Most if not all reporters now have an e-mail address. Getting hold of it if it isn't published might take some doing. But once you have it, simply follow their particular column on page in the paper or magazine and send the occasional complimentary note. Keep it short – none of these people has time to read letters and might get irritated by the imposition on their time.

Inviting a reporter to lunch is one of the best investments you can make.

Of course, if or when you have a legitimate story, they will be happy to entertain you. Some have a generous allowance for just such purposes. If such an opportunity presents itself, make sure that you are a witty and undemanding host. Journalists understand that they are expected to 'sing for their supper' – make them feel appreciated.

There is no hard and fast rule for befriending a worthwhile media contact.

> *The undisputed society gossip supremo in England is Nigel Dempster.*

Lest this author is accused of undue bias, it should be remembered that there was a time when she was the butt of Dempster's devastating satire.

A thoroughly professional hack of the old school, Dempster is one of a dying breed – he is well informed and knows the subjects of his writings

personally. And while he has never hesitated to ridicule the rich and famous when they have deserved it, he is also inherently courteous and can show unexpected kindness and generosity of spirit.
These days Dempster commands more notoriety than some of the people he writes about.

> *It is good form to pretend that one doesn't actually want to be in Dempster's column and to submit to the 'exposure' with a sigh. In truth, most people leak their secrets to Dempster either out of sheer vanity or because they want a controlled 'outing' of their story – in other words, they want to give him their side before anyone else has managed to do it from a different prospective.*

Having married a peer's daughter, he has long been a confidant of the rich, famous and titled, and can make or break a person single-handedly through his half a page column in the *Daily Mail*. He has a passion for racehorses and an appreciation of good wine – mentioned in case you should find yourself the object of his attentions.

ON PARADE

While none is as crucial for the *R&F* hopeful as Dempster's column, there are, of course, other so-called society or gossip pages out there.

UK and US newspaper diaries often swap stories.

Tatler, Vogue and *Harpers & Queen* all have social pages that rival each other in content and pictorial excellence. The lucky editors who record the antics of the *R&F* receive countless invitations and can be powerful allies. A word of caution, though: they have a keen awareness of social status and celebrity quotient. If they perceive that your need for them is greater than theirs for you, you are out before you can spell the title of their publication.

In the United States there is a well-defined line between publications for the rich and famous and scandal sheets that appear at grocery-store checkouts. *The New York Daily News*, the *New York Post*, the *New York Observer* are the newspapers you should aim for.

Then, there are the magazines. New publications

seem to be launched every few months. Access to the well-established ones – *People* magazine, *Vanity Fair* (the grandest of the lot), *Palm Beach Society*, *The Hamptons* magazine – is paved with more hurdles because the celebrity standards are higher. James J. Sheeran, publisher of *Palm Beach Society*, for example, presides over many a charity gala and can do for you on the South East Coast of America what Dempster can do in Britain – turn you into an instant celebrity, or mini-celebrity at the very least.

If you are based in the United States, or harbour social aspirations there, befriend – or establish an advertising/business/sponsor relationship with – Jason Binn, editor of *The Hamptons* and *Gotham magazines*. Both represent essential reading for the aspiring *R&F*. Subscribe to them to get an update on who is who on the social and power circuit and how and where to meet them.

Then, there is the *News of the World* in England, the *National Enquirer* in the US, and sundry magazines devoted to photographing stars and starlets. The latter work mostly in tandem with PRs (OK and Hello are good examples of this) and follow the trends. If one of them develops a fascination with a particular individual (Victoria Beckham for example), the rest follow.

But before you find yourself staring at your smiling face in *OK* or *Hello*, you need to have spent some time inhabiting the scandal sheets of newspapers. Yesterday's news is just that – wrapping paper, as a journalist friend once remarked. Keeping up with fame requires consistent effort.

One person who is particularly good at maintaining his status of major league celebrity – and does so effortlessly – is the Marquess of Bath. But then the marquess has all the attributes of a media myth. He looms large in the public perception, not just because of his unconventional appearance and lifestyle but because the man is an original in the best sense of the word. He is articulate, multi-dimensional, perpetually fascinated by life and seeking to exert his own influence on people's consciousness; he comes across as intriguingly eccentric, even as his duller contemporaries pronounce him a dangerous maverick. If you wish to model yourself on him, you need to truly believe. You have not only to invent a whole new persona for yourself but to believe in it. Of course, if you are attractive and so inclined, you can always apply to become his latest *wifelet* and take a vertiginous, albeit short-lived shortcut to stardom.

> *The seriously wealthy are secretive.*
> *They do not welcome press attention –*
> *rather, they see it as intrusive and*
> *they use their wealth to shield themselves*
> *from the limelight.*

There are several reasons for this – some are personal, others are the common concern of most rich people: one such is that they feel so secure in their status that they are not flattered by the public's fascination, nor do they need the powerful drug it represents; another is the fear of kidnapping.

Patronise Cult Eateries, Clubs, Bars, Shops…

There is an art to patronising trendy venues (and I am not referring here to the truly grand and ruthlessly

ON PARADE

exclusive ones). Fashionable eateries, bars, shops are not clubs but they give the impression of being so. The idea is to make patrons feel special and singled out for their social 'importance'.

Owners of such establishments understand that most people need to belong, and bestowing upon them the privilege of belonging to an inner circle, of sorts, guarantees unswerving loyalty. Inevitably, it is the owner that provides the appeal.

Lady Victoria Hervey used to own Akademi – a boutique in Motcomb Street, London. The entertaining accounts of her weekly antics, in the *Style* supplement of *The Sunday Times*, coupled with her captivating smile and perpetual *joie de vivre*, were largely responsible for pulling the fashionable crowds to Akademi. When her column folded so did Akademi.

Mogens Tholstrup, who created some spectacularly fashionable restaurants, achieved this by gracing the pages of various tabloids himself. Daphne's – his flagship establishment – became the setting of his very public love affairs. He did not invent the formula though. Long before Daphne's turned into a club-like eating venue, the late Peter Langan and Michael Caine presided over the trendy crowds of London at their restaurant, Langan's.

I remember lunching there as an impressionable young girl and asking the waitress to send a bottle of champagne 'to that man over there'. 'You mean Michael Caine? He has a drink already,' came the frosty reply.

Rule number one then – don't ever try to be chummy with the owner if you don't really know him or her.

Maxim's of Paris is another legend – perhaps even the greatest among cult eateries. The favourite dining room of all time for every kind of minor and major celebrity – especially when people still appreciated opulence and elegance – it offers a dream setting with a boudoir-like atmosphere.

My first experience of Maxim's was not an auspicious one. I had booked a table for one over the telephone

ON PARADE

when I turned nineteen. I had prepared for that day and deliberated over my choice of gown for weeks. A teenager's idea of what is stylish and elegant is, of course, a far cry from true distinction. To compound the mistake that my attire represented, I turned up at the famous restaurant's doorstep on foot. Naturally, the maitre d' claimed never to have received my reservation. The lesson was not lost on me and I vowed never to suffer such humiliation again.

Rule number two – never try to jump the gun and head for the top before you have cut your teeth on lesser challenges.

This guide will not presume to list every fashionable restaurant, bar, club or a combination of those – indeed, it is not its purpose to do so. I will cite a few here and there to illustrate a point and apologise in advance to all the marvellous places where I have been made welcome that will not find their names within this narrative.

HOW TO JOIN THE CLUB OF RICH AND FAMOUS

It is impossible to write about cult eateries, however, without mentioning **San Lorenzo** of London and its astonishing enduring power.

Le Laurent in Paris, owned by the late Sir James Goldsmith, has fed a discreet and opulent clientele for years.

The **Louis XV** in Monte Carlo boasts the most ornate dining room and superb cuisine. **The Four Seasons** of New York feeds that city's power brokers.

But few can boast the phenomenal success of San Lorenzo in terms of packing in the rich and famous for decades.

Many a marriage has been proposed there; many a drama has been discreetly presided over by the owners – Mara and Lorenzo Berni.

San Lorenzo is unobtrusively situated in London's Beauchamp Place and serves unassuming food, which is consistently of an excellent quality. But it isn't just the food that attracts scores of regular patrons and

ON PARADE

many more scores of hopefuls to its black door. It is erroneously claimed that the late Diana, Princess of Wales made San Lorenzo what it is. The truth is that Mara and, to a lesser degree, Lorenzo Berni have made **San Lorenzo** the remarkable success it still is and probably will be long after their two children take over.

All of the restaurant's patrons (and if there is an establishment that is run like a club without actually being one, this is it) curry favour with the Bernis. There are several reasons for this. One is Mara's personality. Certainly, she makes everyone feel welcome and special, but so do others who run businesses. There is another quality to Mara Berni's friendship – she comes across as caring and solicitous. She does not shy from offering advice and this can take the form of a bitter pill, but no one takes offence. She is agony aunt, astrologer, confidant, shoulder to cry on, and the perfect person to share your success with – all in one.

The kudos from being recognised and greeted by Mara (who tells all women how pretty, slim, etc,. they are), as well as from her sitting briefly at one's table for a chat, is enormous. In addition to this, there is the compliment that is implicit when you are seated at a good table. There is a pecking order – a fact that she would probably deny – and long-term faithful and famous patrons get seated prominently so they can observe who enters and be observed in turn. There are a couple of large tables for parties and these, too, have an hierarchy to them.

There are those who are genuinely fond of Mara, and there are those who bask in the glory of being seen as personal friends. She is, after all, credited with having offered much emotional support to Diana, Princess of Wales. And it was obvious that she 'mothered' the princess. I have often watched her listening carefully with her face registering concern or delight as the confidence required, and guarding the ladies' room if the princess needed to go there.

It has to be said that even though most of Mara's patrons are both rich and famous (there is perpetually a *paparazzo* or two stalking the door), she dislikes people who have the poor taste to speculate about others' wealth and those who are blatant snobs.

ON PARADE

Dressing down and dining *en famille* are encouraged, and my own children enjoy going there for the atmosphere (they are not treated as a nuisance) and the pasta.

Once the undisputed kings of exclusivity, the gentlemen's clubs of St James's in London have aged somewhat.

*The greatest one of them,
the House of Lords,
has been all but dismantled.*

Then, there is that paragon of good taste and distinction, the night club **Annabel's** and its sister clubs, **Harry's Bar** and **Mark's Club** – all owned by Mark Birley, the famed arbiter of elegance.
Belonging to any or all of the above reflected, and still does to a degree, a social status second to none. It also signifies that one can afford such things.
But the exclusivity has been diluted over the years.

Working on Groucho Marx's premise, 'I don't want to belong to any club that would have me as a member,' many super wealthy individuals set out to conquer the last bastions of the old guard. The *nouveau riche* brought the standards down but injected money into the dwindling fortunes of certain establishments. They put penniless 'titles' on their companies' boards of directors and endeared themselves to sponsors.

I was quite astonished, for example, to see a disgraced city broker lunching at Mark's in the company of a government minister once.

New clubs, more or less exclusive and fashionable, have emerged since. They are run by a new generation, eager to capitalise on rich people's obsession with celebrity. There are celebrity chefs, celebrity girls about town, celebrity columnists, celebrity designers, celebrity mistresses…

To find your way around this maze, dear hopeful *R&F*, you could do worse than find a sponsor to make you a member of **quintessentially.com** – a website run by enthusiastic and super-well-connected new-generation 'titles' (who have a strong family connection with Prince Charles's long-term

ON PARADE

companion, Camilla Parker-Bowles).

Quintessentially eases your way into various clubs, providing you with the access if not with the funds to join. You need several hundred pounds to join quintessentially, but I personally consider it excellent value for the aspiring *R&F*. This is a club that places you immediately in a superior sphere of all that is best in life – that is, all that can be had at a price. It provides a service second to none to those already wealthy and in quest of the absolute best – in any category.

Making it your business to join some or one of these establishments allows you to rub shoulders with those you aspire to emulate, and set yourself well on the way to becoming a fully paid member of that most exclusive of clubs – the *R&F* Club.

Cult shops, hairdressers, style gurus, and so on, are nothing new either. Becoming a client of a designer jewellery shop will place you on that shop's invitation list. Breakfast at **Tiffany's**, **Cartier's** Polo event…the possibilities are

HOW TO JOIN THE CLUB OF RICH AND FAMOUS

exceedingly enticing.

The jeweller of the moment is London-based Stephen Webster, the jewel in whose personal crown is Russian-born wife, Anastasia. Join the list of his clientele and you could get invited to the launching of a new range of silverware, say, or study the ring tray next to a pop star.

Having your hair tinted and cut by **Richard Ward** was the thing last year, and for all I know it still is. If you cannot afford the man himself, just pick any of the mere mortals there – every stylist in the salon is well trained.

Over a cup of coffee you can strike an acquaintance with a Knightsbridge or an Upper Manhattan lady and infiltrate their lunching set. Discover your own designer, stylist, make-up artist and swear by them. Remember, personalities endorse those who offer them free services or frocks, and so on. This is what puts businesses on the map. A PR typically brokers such celebrity endorsements and the hopefuls merely follow.

ON PARADE

Join a Fitness, Country or Sports Club

Wealthy people have an obsession with looking fit.

If they live in a city environment, and do not have a house with its own swimming pool (an impracticality in colder climates), they join one of the more expensive health clubs so they can be secure in the knowledge of treading the mill in good company. Such establishments have proliferated in the last decade or so, and they are becoming more expensive and difficult to join by the year.

There is, for example, the **Home House** club of which one can become a member only if introduced by another, never mind the hefty joining fee. It is rumoured that Madonna is one of its celebrity members; certainly the club received a great deal of press coverage when it opened.

Most grand hotels have a leisure complex, and guests become temporary members when they book a room.

HOW TO JOIN THE CLUB OF RICH AND FAMOUS

Subscriptions to these are hefty, depending on the star rating of the hotel itself. If you can afford the couple of thousand pounds to join, you might be lifting weights next to an investment genius or your next business partner, or sipping juice next to your future husband/wife/lover. Alternatively, you could enjoy a number of visits to different health clubs, without becoming a member, by using your quintessentially membership card (see page 70).

Country clubs are especially expensive and grand in America where membership of them is often part of a compensation package for high-flying business executives. As wealthy Americans tend to live outside of urban areas, most arrange their social lives around their country clubs. But beware – fees in the best establishments there can set you back anything up to $100,000 or more.

Fees for membership of country clubs are comparatively modest in Europe, although by no means cheap. These tend to be social and sports clubs all in one: a golf club, for example, might have social members who do not necessarily play golf but can afford to be members and enjoy the other facilities as well as the company of their peers.

Peter de Savary has long been capitalising on this formula, and the **St James' Clubs** in a number of elegant holiday locations are his brainchild, as is the famous Skibo Castle golf and country club where Madonna and Guy Ritchie chose to tie the knot. It is possible to sample the delights of Skibo Castle even if you are not a member but for a limited number of visits, after which they like you to join – or make a dignified exit.

Shooting clubs in England have suffered as a result of the new weapons law, so their members organise regular jaunts across the Channel where they can practise their sport and also consort with like-minded people. Shooting – like going on safari – is the sport of those who have been brought up with it and can afford it. Not only do you need money to be able to join these rarefied circles, but you need to leave political correctness back home. Your reward, though, is socialising with the cream of society anywhere.

migrate with the jet set

Rich and famous people love to and do travel.

In fact, they spend most of their lives migrating. They do so in private jets, or on cruise liners or their own yachts, but they take commercial flights, too. You can encounter them in VIP lounges to which they get upgraded even if they haven't bought a first-class ticket.

January is the month for travelling to hot climates as it is too cold for skiing. The Caribbean or the Far East, and East or South Africa are desirable destinations. Late February is when the skiing kicks off, and it is to Aspen and Telluride, Val d'Isere, St Moritz, Gstaad, Kloisters and Zermatt that the world's wealthiest individuals flock. They don't go there simply to keep fit – any good snow slope would do for that purpose. They go to these places precisely so that they can move within the confines of their club, meet their peers, and enjoy the après-ski activities.

If you have saved all year for a week in St Moritz for example, and cannot afford even the cheapest room at **Badrutt's Palace**, find a lesser hotel (they do exist, but get booked up almost a year in advance). Make sure you pick a week when there are lots of social activities at **Badrutt's** (they will send you their social calendar on request). There is no point in dining there as most tables are allocated to half-boarders. Do have a pre-dinner drink at the bar, though, and an after-dinner one at the night club as often as every day, unless you decide to devote an evening to the Cresta crowd haunts in town. Dress up – everyone does, unlike the crowd in Aspen where dressing down is the order of the day.

Try to get a temporary membership at the **Corviglia Club**, a very exclusive, if informal establishment on the top of the ski slopes where you are likely to sip broth with every manner of European royalty. Much the same is true of Gstaad, which is more of a private house-party resort. The Palace Hotel there is still a centre of activity, though, as is the Eagle Club. If you can befriend Taki Theodoracopoulos, who is based between New York and Switzerland, you will be on your way up. An absolutely charming man, he could provide you with a passport to the social twirl of celebrities and just plain rich shipowners alike.

March and April are split between skiing and the Bahamas. Palm Beach, Florida, is the small island where the older *R&F* retire, so if you are middle-aged you will feel young by comparison. Not that Palm Beach residents ever allow themselves to get old… They are all of indeterminate age, which should never become a topic of conversation any more than should the number of their marriages. The only give-away to their true age is the elbows.

A very clever man drew my attention to that sad fact one day – a woman can lift her face, her buttocks, her breasts, and so on, but the elbows show wear and tear that cannot be repaired by the surgeon's knife; at least, it isn't an operation anyone has thought of yet.

St Barts in the Caribbean, Nassau and Lyford Cay,

MIGRATE WITH THE JET SET

Florida and California are winter destinations of great attraction for wealthy travellers. You can find inexpensive accommodation in all of these places (or relatively so), but you need to do a lot of homework beforehand. Bear in mind that while drinks at expensive hotels and restaurants are prohibitively costly, the beach is free and an excellent place to flirt or simply make new friendships. Leave the bikini at home if your body is less than perfect, though. A full swimsuit, a wrap and a wide brim hat hide many sins. Do visit **Villa Pasha** in the little-known Abacos (Green Turtle Cay): this is a privately owned villa built on that secluded sandbank that the Cay is. Some super wealthy people sail the Abacos and set anchor in Green Turtle Cay, away from the hustle and bustle of nearby Nassau and garish Paradise Island. **Villa Pasha** is owned by the very charming Paul Thompson, Managing Director of **Lyford Cay Club**.

Most old Palm Beachers congregate in clubs where you cannot become a temporary member – some of the most exclusive rules are still applied there.

The Everglades is at one end of Worth Avenue (the

main shopping street in Palm Beach); the **Colony** hotel is at the other. Between the two lunch, shop, dine and gossip some of the wealthiest and most famous people in America (in addition to many a migrating 'bird').

Dining in the restaurant of the season or having a drink in the latest night club might net you some friends, but if you are serious about Palm Beach you should really consider renting a flat for the season and buying tickets for every benefit gala there is.

This just might bring you to the attention of the editor of the aptly named *Palm Beach Society* magazine, James J. Sheeran. Do not try to compete with the ladies' jewels (unless you can afford to) and the men's cars/polo ponies. Be original instead and resort to period paste ornaments – pins and broaches are very elegant – and simple youthful dresses.

Many *R&F* people, of course, flock to California in the winter. Los Angeles and Beverly Hills are the residential/shopping extensions of Hollywood and, if you have the looks but are not 'discovered' yet, you

MIGRATE WITH THE JET SET

could do worse than spend some time in the movie hub of the world. Jack Nicholson met the mother of his two younger children while she was a waitress there. San Francisco is more sophisticated and quaint and is home to countless Silicon Valley tycoons. Style and originality may be better appreciated there than anywhere else in the Golden State.

April is the month in which the flat racing kicks off in England, so the horsey set returns from Barbados for good. After all, the Monte Carlo Grand Prix is round the corner in May, and there are also the Paris and Milan fashion shows.

The early summer is spent in Europe. In addition to the above, there is the whole season to do in London, with private parties, racing events and fashion shows, as well as countless charity galas and premieres.

Midsummer is always difficult. The south of France has long been a popular destination, but it tends to be overcrowded with tourists at this time of the year. If you can afford to charter a small yacht (Camper & Nicholson have offices in most fabulous locations), head for Sardinia, Portofino, St Tropez and/or the Greek islands.

Beware of the mooring fees. A sailing yacht may not be as comfortable as a motor one, but it creates a better image and it is cheaper if you take fuel costs into account.

You can always drop anchor some distance from the marina and use its facilities on an as-needed basis.

"Isn't it funny how MUCH better champagne tastes when you know that the man giving it to you can REALLY afford it!"

MIGRATE WITH THE JET SET

Many *R&F* retire to country estates during mid-summer or rent villas in Tuscany, or they simply go yachting. Nantucket and Martha's Vineyard, as well as the flashier Hamptons, are the favoured destinations of wealthy Americans, especially those who enjoy sailing.

You can offer to crew there for the season and thus obtain entry to a sailing club. The many social activities on the islands are certain to net a number of friends you would appreciate having. Wealth tends to be conspicuous at the Hamptons and understated on Nantucket Island and the Vineyard. You should consider which fits your personal style better before heading north or south of Connecticut – another watering hole of the wealthy.

The autumn is for visiting exotic places such as Marrakesh or the beaches of North Africa, as well as southern Spain. Majorca and Granada (especially the **Alhambra Hotel**) are ever popular, but one has to know which places to avoid as the exclusive enclaves are well protected and discreet. The **Mamounia Hotel** in Marrakesh is a must, as is the new Kasbah Agafay – a converted fort where you can take a whole group of guests and re-enact Bocaccio's erotic tales from Decameron. **The Palmeraie** resort, built by the Moroccan jetsetter Jaouad Khadiri is the setting of many a fabulous party – as is his **Villa Fandango** restaurant in Casablanca (make sure he is in residence before booking a table).

if all else fails...

Get Courted (or Sued) by a Famous Person

Kiss-and-tell – or kiss-and-sue – is the classic way to take a shortcut to fame and, if you have a good publicist, a lot of cash.

But first you must set your sights on the famous person who might be susceptible to your charms and to whom you might have some access. You could turn delivery boy for the dry cleaners or florist, or become a child's piano tutor. Or you could meet the person while playing tennis, as the former Sophie Rhys-Jones met her prince. I know a flower seller who made his fortune by befriending and later prompting the divorce of a well-known Chelsea lady they have since made a new life in the south of France.

HOW TO JOIN THE CLUB OF RICH AND FAMOUS

Kiss-and-tell has become a huge industry that is profitable both for those who engage in it and for the press: the kiss-and-teller gets a contract along with a cheque, and the newspaper increases its circulation.

Who could possibly forget David Mellor's football T-shirt and the ever more unpalatable revelations of his inamorata, Antonia de Sancha.

Who could ever forget Lady Buck's formidable coup on the steps of the **Dorchester** and her subsequent career as a professional advice-giver on all matters seductive.

It seems that a veritable rash of turgid and often embarrassing revelations about short-lived affairs is saturating the newspaper market at all times. From once venerable cabinet ministers to barely famous TV starlets peddling cringing indiscretions for cash, we are fed a constant diet of that which is best left private.

Then, there is the United States – a land rich in such opportunity. Why, even the President got caught with his pants down – or rather, with the

IF ALL ELSE FAILS...

"Would you like to come up for a drink, or a coffee, or a glass of water — or, — something?"

P.H.

HOW TO JOIN THE CLUB OF RICH AND FAMOUS

evidence all over Miss Lewinsky's infamous
black dress.

Political careers have been destroyed in a single act of
folly – Gary Hart, Senator Kennedy, Jeffrey Archer…
For the women who seduced them and told the world
about it, this has meant a veritable bonanza.

Men play the kiss-and-tell game too, although James
Hewitt – propelled into the realm of minor stardom
because of the late Diana, Princess of Wales's self-
confessed infatuation with him – did not appear to
do quite so well out of it. His book seems to have
vanished from the collective memory as well as from
bookshops, and he has resorted to peddling
her letters.

Even as I write this, there is a pack of reporters
stalking a flat a hundred yards from here, waiting to
catch a glimpse of a celebrity baby. Boris Becker, the
tennis star, unfortunately abandoned his composure
with a half-Russian 'model' (aren't they all…?) who, so
the story goes, went to great and unnatural lengths to
impregnate herself and initiate a paternity suit.

IF ALL ELSE FAILS...

Bullseye Television covered this story from every conceivable angle on behalf of RTL (a German TV channel); and I can certainly testify to that, having been asked to speculate endlessly on how a Russian girl – and a newcomer to boot – would go about becoming rich and famous overnight. I told them to read this book.

Mick Jagger lost the delectable Jerry because of just such a moment of abandon. The only net winner there, as ever is the case, was the mother of his latest (and one hopes) last child, who has not only won a vast financial settlement but been propelled to the ranks of instant if dubious stardom.

If having an affair with a celebrity is unappealing to you, then you can cause them an offence so grave or public that they feel compelled to issue legal proceedings against you. Do remember the slander and libel laws, though... You cannot perpetrate a lie with impunity.

If, however, you express an opinion that is deemed offensive, the proverbial glove might just get thrown in your face, and bingo! you get to face the cameras in front of the Courts of Justice and plead for public support.

I found myself in a similar situation recently – quite unwittingly. A website I published carried a posting on its message board that so upset Elton John and his lawyers that I spent a year in and out of court defending myself against the famous singer. While my predicament was not designed to further my notoriety, it inevitably if regrettably added to it.

Marry into Wealth

Look at Anna Nicole Smith!

I cannot recall the exact size of her fortune by marriage, or rather inheritance on the demise of her very elderly husband, but it makes the mind boggle with its zeros.

I was once asked to marry a decrepit old lecher who had both a title and vast wealth. I was on my third husband at the time, and he was quite rich (all such

IF ALL ELSE FAILS...

"And did you say that you actually owned the Company?"

things being terribly relative, of course), and so I declined. A woman named Susan married him instead and, like Anna Nicole Smith, became a widow shortly after. That I might have been in her shoes, playing 'merry widow', rather than playing hostess to my then husband, never entered my mind at the time.

It is commonly assumed that women are the greater predators when it comes to seeking out rich old men. This isn't the case at all. And I am not talking gigolos here.

I know a man – neither breathtakingly handsome, nor especially witty – who has made a career out of befriending both men and women who just happen to be terminally ill or just plain old.

Now, before you jump to conclusions, he is not in the least bit sinister. I am, in fact, quite sure that he showed great devotion to all his dying friends – which is why they each left him a property. I am greatly heartened by the fact that even though I have not mentioned him in my will he still calls on me occasionally.

But if you are after riches, dear reader, and truly possess no scruples, then go

IF ALL ELSE FAILS...

brighten the last days of an old man, or woman, making sure they have put your name on that most important piece of paper.

The great catches of our times have been laboriously recorded by the press, and it isn't the purpose of this book to list them all here.

Some such marriages – in the old days one used to refer to them as a 'good match' – have resulted in very profitable divorces. The Khashoggi marriage (to Soraya) has an element of the 'Thousand and One Nights' tale to it, what with Soraya's past as a bar hostess and the heady succession of high-class tarts beating the path to Khashoggi's various villas, planes and yachts. Soraya's divorce settlement is veiled in mystery.

Another 'exotic dancer' who married – and divorced – extremely lucratively is Patricia Kluge. Patricia Rose, as she was born, by all accounts began her career as a belly dancer, then progressed to soft-porn movies and Penthouse magazine spreads featuring threesomes, foursomes, and assorted poses in very questionable

HOW TO JOIN THE CLUB OF RICH AND FAMOUS

taste even by today's libertine attitudes. She captured the attentions of media tycoon John Kluge, from whom she was later divorced and pensioned off. She must have had quite a grip on old man Kluge, for her golden handshake was indeed golden.

It was Ivana Trump who coined the phrase, 'Don't get even, get everything.' It is this approach to divorce that has prompted the birth of pre-nuptial agreements, so once you have found your meal ticket you must ensure that you also acquire a good lawyer who can steer you through the maze of financial precautions. This is the place to devote time and attention to detail.

But how do you find a wealthy man or woman and make them want to marry you.

> *For it is the ultimate privilege of wealth to do the bidding – of this you should be aware and prepared for.*

In the preceding chapters we have explored places where one is likely to encounter wealthy individuals. But meeting a rich man or woman is one thing;

IF ALL ELSE FAILS...

captivating them into considering matrimony is another altogether.

Most people born to wealth are bred to apply pathological distrust to the motivations of those that are comparatively penniless. But rich men and women fall in love too. And rich men of a certain age are more likely than not to acquire a 'trophy wife' – someone who is stunning enough, or sufficiently credible, to reflect his own success.

There is no better example in history of such a match than the marriage of Aristotle Onassis and Jacqueline Kennedy. Onassis craved the social status the former First Lady bestowed on him, and she relished the opportunity of amassing a considerable fortune in the process.

How would one set out to woo a wealthy woman? It helps enormously to have the aristocratic looks and demeanour of a Claus von Bulow – famously (or infamously) married to Sunny von Bulow and convicted but acquitted on appeal of her attempted murder. While men like to be perceived as the wealthier of the two partners, the 'breadwinner' as it were, women like to take pride in the achievements of their man. He might be a little-known artist or inventor, or a broker (the latter being a vague description that can mean absolutely anything or nothing at all).

> *Women are notoriously vain. They fall for outrageous flatterers even when aware of being complimented disproportionately.*

The ability to make a woman laugh, physical prowess (the type that does not come from having a lot of muscle, but from inner courage), mental agility, and a plain old-fashioned chivalry (much maligned by those who subscribe to political correctness), are all winners.

Women do not always expect propriety even though they are programmed to be more demure than men. A man needs to be able to identify the moment when he can take the initiative in a relationship. Most men know how to do that instinctively, but they can be intimidated by social superiority or by the wealth of their partner. Wealthy women are essentially lonely unless they have a husband already.

IF ALL ELSE FAILS...

A friend of mine told me once that the late Jackie Onassis remarked to her that she frequently wished that people would call more frequently – instead, they assumed that she was perpetually busy and kept a polite distance.

If you are a man in search of a wealthy partner, one word of caution here – expensively dressed women sitting on the terrace of the Cannes **Carlton Hotel** (or any such place) can be themselves on the lookout for a rich husband, just as a well-groomed, suave man sitting in a hotel lobby can be providing security detail for a rich client. Generally speaking, people with wealth have a quiet confidence about them and do not like drawing attention to themselves. Sending a glass of champagne through the waiter might be refused if you are a total stranger. Better to try sending a flower without pressing your advantage straight away.

> *Most wealthy women long to find a man who devotes his total attention to them.*

They are likely to have been married or born to fathers

who have spent a lifetime building their financial empires and then either dropping dead of a heart attack or eloping with their secretaries.

Apart from the fact that it is bad manners to notice another woman – younger or more attractive – this is especially hurtful to a wealthy woman, who is conditioned to think that she is pursued for her money alone. Make her feel cherished and the only one. It is, without question, more difficult for a penniless man to propose to a woman of means than it is the other way around. You must try to be sincere, guileless and caring. Women are very intuitive and detect insincerity with ease. If you cannot summon up the slightest affection for her, try to find someone else who fits the bill better. Marrying out of desperation is like anything done out of desperation – doomed.

Rich men are, as a rule, not lonely, although there are of course exceptions to this. You need to define your target first of all.

The *nouveau riche*, or those who have made their

fortune as opposed to inheriting it, have a regrettable propensity for showing off. They are generally, albeit not in all cases, brash, loud and obvious. They can be generous to a fault, whereas a 'trust fund baby' – a person living off an inheritance fund – can be positively miserly.

The TFB [trust fund baby] tends to suffer from the inverted snobbery syndrome. For example, he might wear old clothes, drive a battered car, calculate the tip at a restaurant, and barter at every opportunity. Nantucket Island in America is full of such yachtsmen; their attire and general demeanour belie old family wealth. They can be seen messing about on their boats, wearing distressed Nantucket reds (distinctive pink shorts) and weathered hats, snubbing the trendy tourist watering holes in favour of their sailing club or the nearest diner/pizzeria.

European aristocrats are notoriously stingy and there are endless jokes about freezing country houses (although these tend to be exaggerated in my opinion), mended tweed jackets, and penny-pinching practised as a favourite pastime. You really have to embrace their values enthusiastically if you mean to be happy and keep your spouse happy, too.

Typically, the two categories of wealthy men go for different types of women and have different expectations of them.

Splitting wealthy men into two categories may be over simplifying life, but then this is not meant to be a sociological study.

> *The NR [nouveau riche] is more likely to be socially insecure and will try to compensate by seeking a well-born wife – or at least, one who has the manners and poise of someone of impeccable background. Such a wife gives the NR the credibility and circle of friends he craves.*

If he is not concerned with social graces, he will go for a show stopper – a woman with model looks who turns heads at the local bar or pub.

I know a self-made rich man from a Scandinavian country who married a raven-haired beauty wearing such an improbable amount of make-up that the visual impact she created is irrefutable. She is propositioned every now and then but her husband does not take offence – quite the opposite. He is not faithful for all that and considers it his masculine duty to visit topless bars on a regular basis where he entertains equally wealthy clients.

There are no hard and fast rules when trying to capture such a man's attention.

If he thinks you are a catch – i.e., an acquisition to inspire envy among his peers – he might proposition you soon after meeting you. Such men frequent flashy, trendy establishments. Certainly, they follow the trends and they can afford them. They are equally at home in an expensive London club or in Monte Carlo or the Seychelles. They patronise all expensive establishments, shops, and service providers because they can afford to do so and believe that their status requires it of them. You are more likely to meet them on the **Orient Express** than in **Villa d'Este Hotel** on Lake Como, at the **Paris Ritz** than at the **Bristol**, in first-class (or private jets) than in economy, in the latest launched restaurant than in an old established one, and at a promotional/fundraising event than at a private party. To capture their attention, looks, confidence and panache will win the day.

The TFB is more weary, and he is accustomed to meeting his women within his own social circle. You can certainly come across him on the ski slopes of an exclusive resort or while playing golf or riding – *camaraderie* is easily established in a sporting context or in a shared cultural activity. However, you need more attributes than beauty alone to captivate a man of quality as opposed to one that is merely rich. You need to have presence more than physical attractiveness. This is an intangible, I know, and easier to write about than to cultivate. It comes with worldliness and experience and confidence. It requires culture – not necessarily (or not only) academic, but an awareness of the world we live in and an ability to express an original opinion.

You need to know how to dress for a particular occasion so as not to embarrass your suitor, how to address people socially, how to entertain his clients, business associates and friends, how to set a table and to arrange flowers.

You need to have a sense of propriety and know the acceptable level of flirting at a gathering. You need to be able to initiate a conversation, maintain it or change the subject if it causes offence.

Above all, men as well as women do not fail to respond to genuine affection.

Such attributes and many others are generally recognised both by the NR and the TFB and all those who fall in between – and they are appreciated when choosing a mate.

Whether they reciprocate temporarily or for a good long time (or forever), is to a great extent up to you. Every man likes to believe that he is in some way unique. You must absolutely focus your attention on him and never ever scan a room for a more interesting face. Men respond to flattery, too, although of a different nature. They enjoy basking in their women's admiration and they expect their support. Women with careers of their own must understand that most men are programmed to take the steering wheel. Failing to recognise this fact of nature can have dire consequences.

Monotony kills even the most fervent interest. Reinvent yourself, and your romance can renew itself.

Be vivacious, generous of spirit, full of surprises… A shy man is often drawn to a woman with a spirit of adventure; an ebullient one often falls for a steadier, demure woman, perhaps.

The above are not rules – just observations that cannot be applied strictly to individual cases.

In the end, you need to trust in your charm and ability – and have luck on your side.

Commit a Despicable Act and Capitalise on Your Infamy

After all, there is no such thing as bad publicity…

IF ALL ELSE FAILS...

Never has the above adage held more true than in these celebrity cult-obsessed days. Some of the anti-heroes of our times have cashed in on their infamy by way of writing books, doing TV shows, and generally living the life of a fully paid celebrity. While some of their acts have been truly repulsive, others hold great entertainment value.

One such person is surely Lorena Bobbitt, whose act of mutilating a faithless and abusive husband has entered the annals of popular history. The lawyers who managed to keep her out of prison also have the status of media celebrities – and deservedly so. Lisa Kemler (of **Zwerling & Kemler**), one of Lorena's counsel, has a commanding court presence coupled with a very attractive face (the latter is a plus on a TV show). Lisa Kemler's partner, John Zwerling, is another celebrity lawyer, even though he has yet to take up writing Dershowitz style. John Zwerling had me transfixed during one particular cross-examination and closing argument to the extent that I fancied myself at the movies rather than at a real-life trial.

It is said that O.J. Simpson is still looking for the real

killers of his wife. He may be extending the search simply because it is a hugely lucrative one. I have lost track of the number of books and films devoted to this case, and I know that it held most of the wired world spellbound while it lasted on TV. Indeed, not knowing who O.J. was, nor caring particularly, I thought at first that the trial was a fictional drama.

Darius Guppy, that debonair friend of Earl Spencer's, shot into the limelight when he was imprisoned for defrauding an insurance company. Immediately after release he published a book.

Lord Brocket did some time for a similar offence albeit it involved a different commodity. Although he hasn't published a book yet – or perhaps because he hasn't – he gets the frenzied attention of reporters whenever he graces a party. At one such charity event he was monopolised for the entire duration, submitting to a never ending interview with good humour.

Jonathan Aitken, convicted of perjury, has seen more print devoted to his conviction than he ever did for his work as a cabinet minister.

IF ALL ELSE FAILS...

Jeffrey Archer may very well be remembered best for his ill-timed prison diaries. His new publishers, Macmillan, had even ran out of order forms at the last Frankfurt Book Fair. Not only has the now infamous fiction craftsman made a great deal of money – for charity, of course – but he has reinvented himself as a victim of iniquity, without losing his life peerage at that.

Then, there are the insider traders…

Michael Milken did some time, but mostly bailed himself out by handing back some of the fruits of his ingenuity at manipulating the markets. He graces some of the best parties now.

Mark Rich, America's biggest tax evader, has been pardoned by the outgoing President Clinton, 'for donating $100 million to charities'.

Nick Leeson had a film based on his 'breaking' Baring's Bank.

Cynthia Payne and Heidi Fleiss, UK and American madams respectively, shot to prominence during their own trials. Even Christine Keeler, of the Profumo scandal fame, has finally relented and written a book. Her story might not have been well received all those years ago, but times have changed.

The papers, after all, print only what their readers want to read – and it seems that readers will buy the most trivial piece of gossip as long as it pertains to a celebrity. I am not advocating getting into trouble in the pursuit of fame. Far from it.

But if you find yourself in a predicament, try and make the most – or the best – of it.
The world loves a lurid story.

final words of wisdom

How do you proceed once you've acquired the credentials? You have become a familiar face at trendy parties. You are on several PRs' invitation lists, and you get your picture in social columns. You have metamorphosed into a stylish 'swan' and have an enviable set of friends.

Unless you have married a movie or pop star, or won the lottery, you need to consider how to put the above achievements to use in order to become truly wealthy. No doubt your new circle of acquaintances will include stock market professionals or simply investment wizards. Avail yourself of their expertise and connections.

A well-placed word can go a long way towards funding your business venture. Follow the savvy stock market investor. Charm your way into joining someone else's project.

Society girl about town Tara Palmer-Tomkinson moved briefly to the business pages of newspapers after being invited to mastermind the running of a hotel.

Keep alert and open to suggestions. Property deals have made many a millionaire within a short period of time. Protect your newly acquired wealth and make it grow. Wealthy individuals spend a great deal of time and effort in protecting their fortune: from the taxman; from the fluctuations of interest rates, currencies and property values; from death duties and inheritance tax.

With this guide in mind, and for the purpose of educating myself further on the subject, I recently accepted an invitation to attend a seminar organised by the St James's Place Group. The St James's Place Group was founded in 1991 under the name of J. Rothschild Assurance Group, its parent company having been originally established by Lord Rothschild. This being a name synonymous with wealth, I told myself that there could be no better custodians of one's assets – whether liquid or property.

FINAL WORDS OF WISDOM

Appropriately enough, the subject of this seminar was 'Investment strategy and Inheritance Tax Planning'. One of the partners held the audience absolutely riveted for the best part of some two-and-a-half or three hours. Guiding us through the maze of financial services and their sundry providers, interacting with participants, and illustrating various points on a screen, he sent a potent message – manage it or lose it!

Do not be intimidated, dear reader, by the opulence of the group's headquarters in Hamilton Place, London, nor by the name of its founder. While many of its clients are super wealthy, the moderately so might find themselves joining the former category by entrusting their savings to one of these hand-picked financial advisors (who are invited to join the group, we were told, as one might be by an exclusive club).

The message was clear: keep your money in a bank and see it diminish in terms of purchasing power as interest rates lose the race against inflation rates.

Fail to make a will and the taxman will make it for you – at the expense of your beneficiaries. The one thing that registered the most, however, was the ingenuity of the concepts, each and every one designed to make you richer. Not only were the audience able to ask any questions, but they were also treated to lunch after the talk, thus giving them the opportunity to exchange thoughts – and cards. Unobtrusively and charmingly the speaker joined different tables and dealt with remaining queries. If you've reached your goal and joined the ranks of the rich if not quite yet famous – or even if you are halfway there – your prospects might be much improved by taking financial advice from such a company.

There are, of course, many other ways of making a fortune and of arresting the imagination of the public.

You could be the next Internet tycoon or the next girl to be embraced by the editors of super trendy *New York* magazines.

You could capture on film the picture that every newspaper editor would die (or pay millions) for. Or, having captured the picture, you could become a publishing director yourself. You might find yourself

FINAL WORDS OF WISDOM

living next door to the Marquesa di Varela, who *used* to interview for *Hello* magazine.

You could lose a major libel case, yet win great public and media support, as did the Count Nikolai Tolstoy – or you can bask in the reflected glory of such a relative.

You could become an overnight pop star – singing skills are not essential.

You could try wear a dress as tacky as Liz Hurley's (the famous pin dress) at an event where there is a lot of press, and hope that you get noticed without having Hugh Grant as an accessory.

You could write a bestseller – and many undiscovered authors have.

Notoriety, however, can haunt you, winking irreverently at you through the satirical video art compilations of Phillip Patiris *(www.moderntv.com)*. If you've been on television long enough, chances are you will have become the butt of his sardonic wit and seen your grotesque self immortalised in a message particular to the producer.

Patricia Rose's soft-porn photographs were such an embarrassment when she married media tycoon John Kluge that he took the extraordinary step of purchasing the rights to most of them so that they could not be republished. Her image is indelibly associated with her past history.

Profumo never quite recovered from the 1960s sex scandal and devoted the rest of his life to charitable works.

The late Diana, Princess of Wales may have wished that she did not give THAT television interview…

The Duchess of Argyll, in her last years, tried to live down the story of her divorce and the Duke citing a multitude of men as her lovers. She denounced the exaggerated accounts of her affairs in conversation with me and sought to whitewash history.

Fame is fickle. There is nothing so obsolete as yesterday's news.

FINAL WORDS OF WISDOM

Cast your mind back and try to remember all the names that have graced the front pages for days, weeks, months – and then vanished without a trace. Princess Diana is a perfect example. Once the most photographed face on Earth, her image is no longer sufficient to rescue the ailing finances of the charitable trust founded in her name; and Diana memorabilia no longer sells.

Rich people die too – and can suffer poor health that no amount of money can alleviate. It is, of course, preferable to suffer in comfort than to suffer in poverty and misery. But wealth does not buy good health.

Finally, happiness can be achieved without great fortune or fame. For most, it is reflected in the smile of a loved one or of one's children. But if you are fortunate enough to attain them, little else beats the taste of fame and fortune.

Go for it.

The Party Bible

"A master class in the ritz, blitz and glitz of entertaining"
Ivana Trump

Liz Brewer

Liz Brewer represents some of the really rich and famous. She has advised, befriended, promoted and in some cases made many an A list name. An eminence grise of the party circuit, she regularly appears on TV chat shows elucidating the finer points of etiquette and entertaining. Irrespective of budget, her precise and definitive breakdown of every facet of entertaining makes her a book a must-read for every existing or would-be hostess. **The Party Bible** distils her 25 years of experience into a 144 page master class. It is also richly illustrated with hitherto unpublished photographs of some of her most memorable events and partying celebrities

"The Midas touch of the party world." **Dame Shirley Bassey**

ISBN 1 903906 19 9

Glossy Paperback

£16.99

144 pp 210mm x 220mm

HOW TO FLIRT AND BE SEDUCTIVE

Valentina Artsrunik

The arts of flirting and seduction have evolved in response to civilise the most powerful, compulsive and primeval instinct in man – mating and reproduction. As is the case with all such rituals, the rules and protocols have developed over the ages but the basic steps of what Chaucer called ye olde dance of the worlde are timeless. This tongue-in-cheek guide explores what makes some people better dancers than others: how they do; what moves, props and scripts work best... In so learning, perhaps one can also learn to harness rather than to be driven by the emotions of love and sex: infatuation, obsession, jealousy, passion...

ISBN 1 903906 02 4

April 2003

Paperback

£7.99

HOW TO HANDLE A COMPULSIVE PHILANDERER

Valentina Artsrunik

Whatever the reasons, men womanise more than women manise, although it is a moot point why the two do not equal out. After all, who are the men womanising with if not with other women? Well, they may not be womanising but certainly they do philander more with their own sex than do women. They also consort with prostitutes, consume more pornography and fantasise more about extra-marital sex than do women. The author casts an elegant eye over this eternal problem for women and comes up with some witty, intriguing but also practical solutions.

ISBN 1 903906 12 1

June 2003

Paperback

£7.99

112pp

156mm x 131mm

HOW TO DRINK AND DRIVE WITHOUT GETTING CAUGHT... OR CAUSING AN ACCIDENT

John McVicar

A spoof book with a real message!

Some drivers regard drinking 'n' driving as their sovereign right. There are countless publications that go to why they shouldn't, **How to Drink and Drive** is the first one that analyses how to do it safely. This is the definitive guide to the law and its loopholes, but also what the intoxicated driver should know and do to minimise the risk of causing an accident when out of his head.

ISBN 1 903906 06 7

August 2003

Paperback

£7.99

112pp

156mm x 131mm

CUTTING EDGE

The latest advances in cosmetic surgery
Dr. Nick Serdev, MD, PhD

In this guide published by Artnik, Dr Serdev provides in layman's terms what amounts to an overview of the latest methods in cosmetic surgery. It gives the reader a road map of information on state-of-the-art surgical skills and the pros and cons of particular forms of treatment including breast enhancement surgery, body sculpturing, liposculpture, rhinoplasty, face lifts, facial rejuvenation and so on.

Techniques in "beautification surgery" are undergoing what amounts to a sea change in advancement.

In 2003, the International Academy of Cosmetic Surgery holds its annual conference at the Riviera Holiday Club on the Black Sea. It is organised by Dr Serdev and attended by such luminaries in the field as Dr. Ivo Pitangui and Dr. Pierre Fournier among others.

ISBN 1 903 906229

August 2003

Paperback

£7.99

112pp

156mm x 131mm